AF575906

VOICES

Roberta Baxter

2001 SW 31st Avenue
Hallandale, FL 33009
www.mitchelllane.com

First Edition, 2021.

Author: Roberta Baxter
Designer: Ed Morgan
Editor: Sharon F. Doorasamy

Little Mitchie is an imprint of Mitchell Lane Publishers.

Title: Musical Instruments Around the World: Voices / by Roberta Baxter
Description: Hallandale, FL :
Mitchell Lane Publishers, [2021]

Series: Instruments Around the World
Library bound ISBN: 978-1-68020-600-5
eBook ISBN: 978-1-68020-601-2

Photo credits: pp. 4-5 Spencer Imbrock on Unsplash, pp. 6-7 Album / Prisma/Newscom, pp. 8-9 freepik.com, pp. 10-11 Fine Art Images Heritage Images/Newscom, pp. 12-13 Album/Newscom, p. 14 Fred de Noyelle / Godong/picture alliance / Godong/Newscom, p. 15 Jens B'ttner/dpa/picture-alliance/Newscom, pp. 16-17 freepik.com, p. 18 Image Press Agency/Sipa USA/Newscom, PARAMOUNT PICTURES / Album/Newscom, p. 19 Jason L Nelson/AdMedia/Newscom, U.S. Air Force, Heinrich Klaffs CC-BY-SA-2.0, VINCENT WEST/REUTERS/Newscom, pp. 20-21 freepik.com

CONTENTS

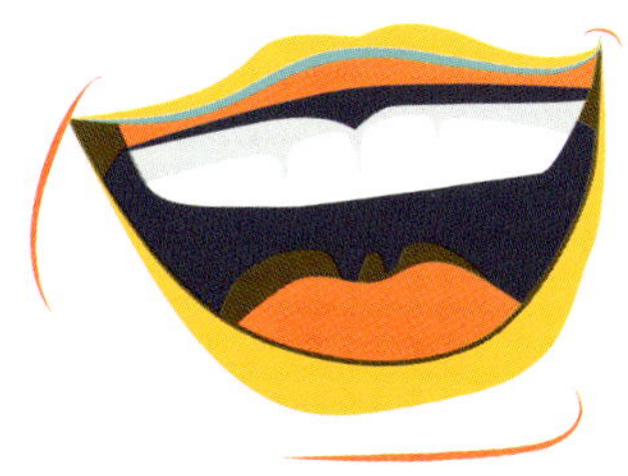

Words in **bold** can be found in the Glossary.

People everywhere love music. Sometimes people play **instruments**. Other times, the music is singing.

6

Anthropologists believe the human voice may be the oldest musical instrument. The common ancestor of modern humans had the vocal **anatomy** to sing at least 530,000 years ago. But it is impossible to know if they did.

Singing begins with breathing. The breath goes out through the **voice box** or **vocal cords**. The voice box is a set of thin muscle fibers in your throat. Air passes over the muscle fibers. The fibers vibrate and make sound. Voices can sing from low to high notes.

Hieroglyphs from ancient Egypt show people singing and playing instruments. **Archaeologists** found 3,400-year-old clay tablets with a song called "Hurrian Hymn No. 6" in the ancient Syrian city of Ugarit. It is considered the world's oldest melody.

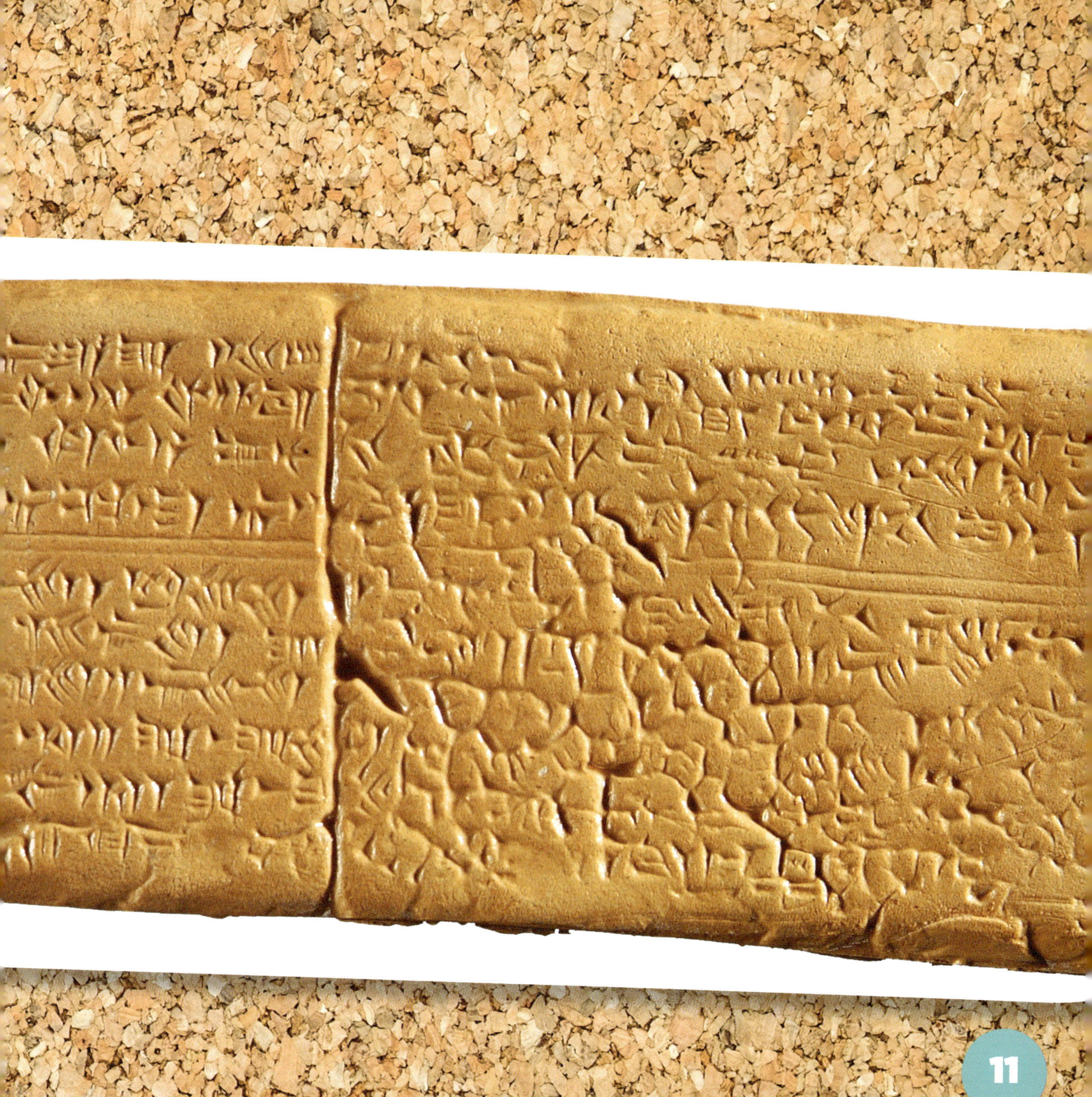

Classical music in India dates back to vocal chants from sacred scriptures more than 6,000 years old. Ancient Greeks and other cultures used singing as part of their religion. The word music comes from one of the daughters of the mythological Greek god Zeus.

GREECE
INDIA

People called troubadours traveled around Europe starting about 1100 AD. They sang songs and played **lutes** from town to town. Singing was also used in worship services.

About 500 years ago, a new kind of vocal music started. It is called opera. It began in Italy. Operas tell a story through singing. Singers act out the parts of the story and sing.

A person can sing alone or in a choir, chorus, trio, quartet, or band. Some singers use instruments to accompany their voices, while others only use their voice.

The list of famous singers is endless.

DEAN
MARTIN
JUDY
GARLAND
FRANK
SINATRA
TAYLOR
SWIFT
LUCIANI
PAVAROTTI
ARETHA
FRANKLIN

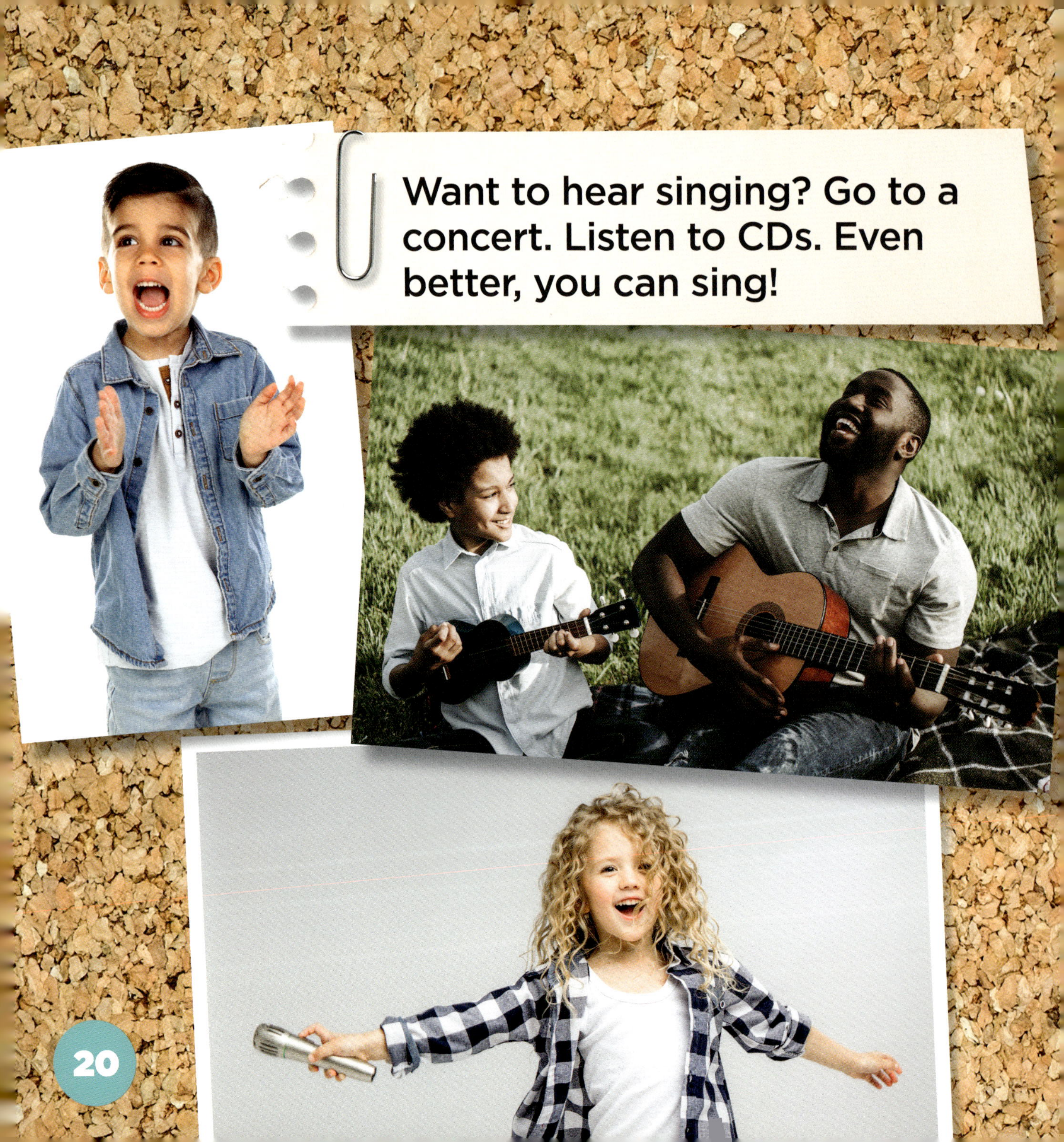

Want to hear singing? Go to a concert. Listen to CDs. Even better, you can sing!

EXPERIMENT WITH YOUR VOICE

You can already sing songs. Try something different. Here are some experiments with your voice.

1. Sing a note and see how high you can go. Then see how low a note you can sing. Try it with a friend to see who can sing higher or lower.
2. Sing in a shower. The small space will make your voice sound different.
3. If you have long hair, tie it back before you try this experiment. Then sing notes into a turning fan. What do you think of that sound?
4. Hold a straw in your mouth and sing a song. How does that sound compare to regular singing?

WHERE TO FIND FREE, USED, OR INEXPENSIVE INSTRUMENTS

- **Ask your teacher.**
- **Talk to your grandparents.** They might have some in their homes.
- **Ask the music director** at your **church**, **synagogue**, **temple**, or **mosque**.
- **Go with your parents** to **yard sales**, **flea markets**, and **secondhand shops**.
- **Ask your parents** to check **Internet websites** for discounted instruments.
- **Contact your local symphony** or a **local charity** that supports music programs.

GLOSSARY

anatomy
The body of a person or living thing

anthropologist
Someone who studies human development and society or different societies

archaeologist
Someone who studies old cultures and objects

hieroglyphs
Pictures or symbols used as writing in ancient Egypt

instrument
An object that produces music when played by a person

lute
A stringed instrument, similar to the guitar, used in the 1400s

voice box
The part of the throat that holds the vocal cords

vocal cords
Thin muscle fibers that produce sounds for speaking or singing

FURTHER READING

Landau, Elaine. *Is Singing For You?* Lerner Publications, 2013.

Russell-Brown, Katheryn. *A Voice Called Aretha*. Bloomsbury Children's Books, 2020.

Sammy, CeCe. *If You Can Speak You Can Sing*. Eyewear Publishing, 2019.

INDEX

ABOUT THE AUTHOR

ROBERTA BAXTER played an instrument in the school band and sang in the chorus. She enjoys singing at church. She lives in Colorado and has published numerous nonfiction books for students of all ages.